To Kiff Wallace

Second Book of Trumpet Solos

*Zweites Spielbuch für
B-Trompete und Klavier*

edited and arranged for B♭ trumpet and piano by

JOHN WALLACE
and
JOHN MILLER

Faber Music Limited
London

Contents : Inhalt

© 1985 by Faber Music Ltd
First published in 1985 by Faber Music Ltd
Bloomsbury House
74–77 Great Russell Street
London WC1B 3DA
Cover design by Roslav Szaybo and Studio Gerrard
Printed in England by Caligraving Ltd
All rights reserved
ISBN10: 0-571-50857-X
EAN13: 978-0-571-50857-0

To buy Faber Music publications or to find out about the full range of titles available
please contact your local music retailer or Faber Music sales enquiries:

Faber Music Limited, Burnt Mill, Elizabeth Way, Harlow, CM20 2HX England
Tel: +44 (0)1279 82 89 82   Fax: +44 (0)1279 82 89 83
sales@fabermusic.com   fabermusicstore.com

Preface

Second Book of Trumpet Solos is for the player who already has a firm grasp of basic technique and is keen to develop his or her playing skills further. The pieces are arranged in order of increasing technical difficulty, and the ground they cover is equivalent to Associated Board (U.K.) Grades 5-7.

As in *First Book of Trumpet Solos*, we have tried to choose material that will be enjoyable, and not just challenging, to play. So while there is once again a strong didactic thread running through our selection, we hope that the wide variety of composers, styles and periods represented will sustain the player's musical interests as well as fostering technical development.

At the end of the book we have added notes on technique and performance for every piece. These should be taken as hints and suggestions rather than instructions!

JOHN WALLACE
JOHN MILLER

Vorwort

Das *Zweite Spielbuch für Trompete und Klavier* ist für Spieler gedacht, die die Grundtechniken schon gut beherrschen und ihr spielerisches Können erweitern wollen. Die Stücke, angeordnet nach zunehmendem Schwierigkeitsgrad, eignen sich für Spieler mit mindestens zwei Jahren Praxis.

Wie im *Ersten Spielbuch für Trompete und Klavier* haben wir versucht, Material zu sammeln, daß nicht nur eine Herausforderung beim Spiel bietet, sondern auch Spaß macht. Wir hoffen deshalb, daß, während sich auch hier wieder ein starker didaktischer Faden durch die Sammlung zieht, die Auswahl der vertretenen Komponisten, Stilrichtungen und Perioden sowohl das musikalische Interesse der Spieler gefangen hält, als auch ihre Entwicklung fördert.

Am Ende des Buches haben wir Anmerkungen zur Technik und Darbietung für jedes Stück angefügt. Diese sollten eher als Vorschläge und nicht so sehr als Anweisungen betrachtet werden!

JOHN WALLACE
JOHN MILLER
Deutsche Übersetzung: Helga Braun

1. DER SCHMIED

The Blacksmith

Johannes Brahms
(1833–1897)

2. GILES FARNABY'S DREAME

Giles Farnabys Traum

Giles Farnaby
(*c.* 1563–1640)

3. HET SNEEKER KLOKSPEL

The Bells of Sneek · Die Glocken von Sneek

Anon. (Dutch)

4. VOIS-TU LA NEIGE QUI BRILLE?

Do you see the glistening snow? · *Siehst du den glitzernden Schnee?*

Jean–Baptiste Arban
(1825–1889)

5. MAPLE LEAF RAG

Ahornblatt-Rag

Scott Joplin
(1868–1917)

Tempo di marcia (♩= 76)

6. VOLUNTARY

Orgelsolo

Sanders Dupuis
(1733-1796)

7. THE HUNTING PARTY

Die Jagdgesellschaft

Johann Nepomuk Hummel
(1778-1837)

D.C. al fine

8. PRELUDE

Fryderyk Chopin
(1810-1849)

9. HALLING

Edvard Grieg
(1843-1907)

10. PRELUDE

Alexander Nikolayevich Skryabin
(1872–1915)

11. CHANSON NAPOLITAINE

Neapolitan Song · Neapolitanisches Lied

Pyotr Il'yich Tchaikovsky
(1840–1893)

12. PRELUDE

Fryderyk Chopin
(1810–1849)

13. MARCHE

Anon.
(1725)

14. THE NOBLE SAVAGE

Der edle Wilde

Johann Nepomuk Hummel
(1778-1837)

15. THE MOOSE IS LOOSE

Der Elch ist los

John Wallace
(1949-   )

Energico (♩ = 126)

16. PRELUDE

Alexander Nikolayevich Skryabin
(1872–1915)

17. BALLAD OF THE SOUTHERN ESKIMO

Ballade des südlichen Eskimos

John Wallace
(1949–   )

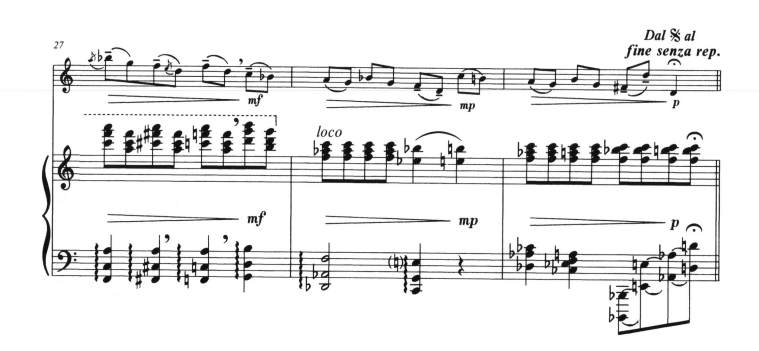

18. IDYLLE

Edward Elgar
(1857-1934)

1. Although his last two symphonies come from the same period as the first two of Mahler (the late 19th century), Brahms was extremely conservative in matters of orchestration, and wrote for the trumpet and horn as though they were still 'natural' (ie. valveless) instruments. Nevertheless, his parts are very satisfying to play. This song by Brahms is well-suited to adaptation for trumpet, since its melodic line is very close in style to that of his orchestral trumpet parts. Launch straight into the music and fill the instrument with air. Let the air do the work of producing a bright, golden tone. Think of the leaps in pitch as part of a continuous flow, and phrase them together – don't 'attack' each note in isolation with an over-vigorous tongue. The last five bars of the trumpet line have been added by the arranger, and are borrowed from the posthorn part of Mozart's Serenade, K.320.

2. This piece (from the *Fitzwilliam Virginal Book*) will look easy on paper, but you may find that its long, quiet phrases make considerable demands on your breath control. Try to play the first four bars in one breath (it may take time to build up to this, but it *is* possible!), starting the second phrase (beginning at bar 5) 'on the breath', that is, with very little or no tongue. Note that a 'speaking breath' will often go much further than you imagine; the deepest breath possible is not necessarily the best preparation for sustained playing at a quiet dynamic.

3. This piece will work well at a variety of tempos, but whatever tempo you eventually play it at, the essential skill here is the accurate placing of individual notes in different registers, and this demands SLOW practice!

4. From Arban's *Cornet method*. Aim for a relaxed, *legato* style of playing and a sweet, well-focused sound. The ornaments should not stand out but should sound like a natural and integral part of each musical phrase.

5. Rags are often played too fast. The feeling here should be gentle rather than insistent, so keep the tempo steady. Do not use too hard a tongue, or the piece will sound 'clipped'.

6. This piece was originally written for the organ. The effect should be rather grand and stately, but don't force the tone; just concentrate on producing a bright, ringing sound and articulate each note crisply. Pay special attention to the dotted rhythms; don't allow them to become triplets!

7. The first of two extracts in this volume from Hummel's *Indian Rondo*, originally for piano (see also *First Book of Trumpet Solos*, no.24). Hummel's tuneful, rather theatrical music suits the trumpet very well. His most celebrated use of the instrument is in the famous Trumpet Concerto, but it also has a prominent role in two of his chamber works, the Grand Military Septet and a Trio, now lost, for violin, keyed trumpet and piano. If the missing Trio ever comes to light, it is to be hoped that it will include music as immediate in its appeal, with as much vitality and melodic inventiveness as *The Hunting Party*. Make the opening bold and confident (place the first three notes like the opening of the Haydn Trumpet Concerto!), with as great a contrast as possible for the central section (from bar 17).

8. Learning to play a sustained, chorale-like melody smoothly and with soft production is essential on the trumpet. Also essential for the trumpet-player is careful planning of dynamics. The effect of an unrestrained *fortissimo* at the opening of this piece would be very unmusical; what is needed here is a full, rich, dark sound.

Try to blend with the piano – imagine that the chords underneath your melody line are being played by the rest of the brass section!

9. Norway's most characteristic dance, akin to the Scottish 'reel'. This piece provides useful exercise for the fingers, especially the under-used third finger! A gradual *accelerando* on the repeat, adding to the excitement of the dance, is permissible.

10. Originally a piano piece for the left hand alone, this Prelude in a Chopinesque manner comes from Skryabin's early period. Be aware of the relation between the character of the music and the sort of sound you want to produce. At bar 13, your playing should become fiery and passionate, but in bars 17 and 18 you should allow your tone colour to soften, melting back to the limpid melancholy of the main theme at bar 19.

11. This dance occurs in Tchaikovsky's famous ballet *The Sleeping Beauty*, where it is written for Cornet in A. Aim for clarity of articulation and lightness of touch. The *più mosso* section (from bar 37) should not be played at too fast a tempo; remember that it was originally danced to.

12. If you can achieve purity of tone and evenness of line at a low dynamic in this beautiful, seamless melody, it will stand you in good stead when you come to tackle original trumpet compositions such as the slow movement of Hummel's Trumpet Concerto. Do not take in too much air at the beginning; you can achieve perfect control, without discomfort, by taking smaller 'sips' of air throughout the piece.

13. This piece is amongst the most technically challenging in the collection. Practise it slowly until it flows. Only then increase the tempo.

14. From Hummel's *Indian Rondo*. On the B♭ trumpet, A♭ major is a mellow, resonant key for sustained melodic playing. Be aware of this as you play, and feel the tempo in a slow two beats to the bar (*alla breve*) rather than a faster four; this will free the melody and let it take wing, so to speak. The trills in bars 3, 5, 7, 13 and 15 should be 'measured'; possible solutions are

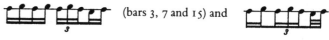 (bars 3, 7 and 15) and (bars 5 and 13). The central section must sound effortless (even though it may not be!). Try to play the triplet passage-work *leggiero*. The secret is to train the tongue to activate the sound with the smallest of movements; in this way, fast repetitions will not disturb the embouchure. Mouthpiece pressure should be as light as possible; any lessening of responsiveness caused by numbing of the lips will adversely affect your sound.

15. A tongue-tester! Rather than extreme speed, aim for accuracy of pitch and precision of articulation. Tonguing at the tip of the teeth should help this. Try both fast single-tonguing and slow double-tonguing; it is important to have an 'overlap' in tonguing speeds, so that you are never caught out by a medium-fast passage in the 'gap' between the two types of articulation. In the low register passages, be careful that the tongue does not open the lip aperture too much; this will send the pitch flat. (Supporting the diaphragm with the stomach muscles should also be helpful.)

16. Skryabin's Prelude, op.67 no.1, though quiet and restrained throughout, uses the same harmonic language and lives in the same mystical, ecstatic world as the composer's well-known

Poem of Ecstasy, one of the major landmarks in the orchestral trumpet repertoire. Technically speaking, this Prelude is an exercise in *legato*, breath control, and playing to the extremes of *pianissimo* and *dolcissimo*. A soft fibre mute is recommended.

17. A fun piece, inspired by the trumpet-writing of American composer George Gershwin. Don't be afraid, in music of this type, of 'warming' your sound with a controlled *vibrato*. The first section is lyrical, and its melody must unfold seamlessly. Nonetheless, you should at the same time be counting quavers meticulously, so that you can fit exactly with the important piano part. In the second section (from bar 15), move the tempo forward and give free rein to an expressive *rubato*. Give a clear lead to the pianist; it's his turn to follow now!

18. Elgar's melodies are particularly well-suited to the cornet, and you should aim here for a sweet, singing, cornet-like tone. Remember that one of Elgar's favourite markings for brass passages was *nobilmente*, but be aware also that his melodic writing calls for subtle nuances of expression. Accentuation marks can mean different things in different periods; the *sforzando* in bar 34 indicates poignant emphasis rather than a sudden, forceful accent.

---

1. Brahms war, obwohl seine beiden letzten Symphonien aus der gleichen Zeit stammten wie die beiden ersten von Mahler (spätes 19. Jh.), ausgesprochen konservativ, was den Orchestersatz angeht, er schrieb für Trompete und Horn, als seien sie immer noch 'natürliche' (d.h. ventillose) Instrumente. Aber es ist dennoch sehr befriedigend, seine Stücke zu spielen. Dieses Brahmsche Lied eignet sich vorzüglich für eine Bearbeitung für die Trompete, da dessen Melodieführung dem Stil seiner Trompetenstücke für Orchester sehr ähnlich ist. Man sollte sich direkt in die Musik hineinstürzen und das Instrument mit Luft füllen. Diese sollte arbeiten und helle, goldene Töne hervorbringen. Die Höhensprünge sollte man sich als Teil eines ununterbrochenen Flusses vorstellen und sie miteinander verbinden und sich nicht mit überanstrengter Zunge an jede Note einzeln ranmachen. Die letzten fünf Takte der Trompetenmelodie sind vom Bearbeiter angefügt worden, sie sind aus der Posthornpartie von Mozarts Serenade, K.320 entliehen.

2. Dieses Stück (aus dem *Fitzwilliam'schen Virginal Book*) mag auf dem Papier einfach erscheinen, aber seine langen, ruhigen Phrasen stellen große Ansprüche an die Atemkontrolle des Spielers. Man versuche die ersten vier Takte mit einmaligem Atemholen zu spielen (es mag eine Weile dauern, bis man dies erreicht, aber es *ist* möglich!), und beginne die zweite Phrase (ab Takt 5) 'auf dem Atem', d.h. mit wenig oder gar keiner Zungenarbeit. Man sollte nie vergessen, daß der 'Sprechatem' oft sehr viel weiter reicht, als man sich vorstellt; der tiefste Atemzug ist nicht unbedingt die beste Vorbereitung für ein anhaltendes Spiel mit ruhiger Dynamik.

3. Dieses Stück klingt bei den unterschiedlichsten Tempi gut, aber welches Tempo auch immer gewählt wird, das eigentliche Können liegt im exakten Setzen der einzelnen Töne in den verschiedenen Tonlagen, und das erfordert langsames Üben!

4. Aus Arbans *Kornettmethode*. Man sollte ein ausgeglichenes *Legatospiel* anstreben und einen sanften, klaren Ton. Die Verzierungen sollten in jeder musikalischen Phrase wie ein natürlicher, integrierter Teil klingen.

5. Rags werden oft zu schnell gespielt. Die Stimmung sollte hier eher sanft als nachdrücklich sein, man halte das Tempo dementsprechend ruhig. Nicht mit zu starkem Zungenschlag spielen, sonst klingt das Stück 'abgehackt'.

6. Dieses Stück wurde ursprünglich für die Orgel geschrieben. Der Effekt sollte ziemlich großartig und feierlich, die Stimmung aber nicht erzwungen sein, man konzentriere sich darauf, einen leichten und glockenklaren Klang hervorzubringen und spiele jede einzelne Note scharf und deutlich. Man achte besonders auf die Stakkatorhythmen und lasse sie nicht zu Triolen werden!

7. Der erste der beiden Auszüge aus Hummels *Indisches Rondo* in diesem Band war ursprünglich für Klavier gesetzt (vgl. *Erstes Spielbuch für Trompetensolos*, Nr.24). Hummels melodische, ziemlich dramatische Musik eignet sich hervorragend für die Trompete. Sein wohl anerkanntestes Stücke für dieses Instrument ist sein berühmtes Trompetenkonzert, aber sein Kammerwerk, das Große Militärseptett und ein inzwischen verlorengegangenes Trio für Geige, Klappentrompete und Klavier spielen ebenfalls eine herausragende Rolle. Sollte das verlorene Trio je wieder aufgefunden werden, so hofft man, daß es eine Musik enthält, die so unmittelbar im Ausdruck und von so großer Lebensfreude und musikalischer Phantasie ist wie *Die Jagdgesellschaft*. Man beginne das Stücke stark und selbstbewußt (spiele die ersten drei Noten wie die Eröffnung von Haydns Trompetenkonzert!) und zeige den Gegensatz zu dem Mittelteil (ab Takt 17) so deutlich wie möglich.

8. Es ist überaus wichtig für den Trompetenspieler, eine verhaltene, choralartige Melodie weich und mit sanftem Spiel gestalten zu lernen. Von gleich großer Wichtigkeit ist exakte Planung der Dynamik. Ein unbeherrschtes *fortissimo* bei der Eröffnung dieses Stücks böte einen unmusikalischen Effekt; was wir hier brauchen, ist ein voller, reicher, dunkler Klang. Man versuche, mit dem Klavier zu harmonisieren – man stelle sich vor, daß die Töne unterhalb der eigenen Melodie von den übrigen Blechbläsern gespielt werden!

9. Der berühmteste Tanz Norwegens ist mit dem schottischen 'reel' verwandt. Dieses Stück bietet eine nützliche Fingerübung, ganz besonders für den wenig benutzten dritten Finger! Es ist gestattet, die Wiederholung langsam schneller werden zu lassen, um dem Tanz Spannung zu verleihen.

10. Dieses Präludium im Stile Chopins, ursprünglich ein Klavierstück für die linke Hand, stammt aus Skryabins früher Periode. Man vergegenwärtige sich ständig die Beziehung zwischen dem Charakter der Musik und der Art des Klanges, die man erreichen will. Bei Takt 13 sollte das Spiel feurig und leidenschaftlich werden, aber bei Takt 17 und 18 sollte die Klangfarbe wieder weicher werden und bei Takt 19 zu der klaren Melodie des Hauptthemas zurückschmelzen.

11. Dieser Tanz stammt aus Tschaikovskys berühmten Balett *Dornröschen* und wurde für das Kornett in A-Dur geschrieben. Klarer

Ausdruck und ein leichter Ton sollten angestrebt werden. Der *più mosso* Teil (ab Takt 37) sollte nicht zu schnell gespielt werden; man halte in Erinnerung, daß ursprünglich dazu getanzt wurde.

12. Wenn es dem Spieler gelingt, Klarheit des Klanges und ebenmäßigen Melodiefluß mit geringem Kräfteaufwand in dieser schönen, geschlossenen Melodie zu vereinen, wird ihm dies dienen, wenn er sich an Originalkompositionen für die Trompete, wie z.B. den langsamen Satz aus Hummels Trompetenkonzert macht. Zu Beginn nicht zu tief einatmen; perfekte Kontrolle kann ohne Unbequemlichkeit erreicht werden, indem man das ganze Stück durch kleinere "Luftschlucke" nimmt.

13. Dieses Stück gehört zu den technisch anspruchsvollsten in der Sammlung. Langsam üben bis der Melodiefluß erreicht ist. Erst dann sollte das Tempo erhöht werden.

14. Aus Hummels *Indisches Rondo*. Auf der B-Trompete ist As Dur eine reife Tonart für eine getragene Melodie. Man sollte sich dies beim Spiel immer vor Augen halten und das Tempo langsam und auf zwei Schlägen je Takt (*alla breve*) statt schneller und auf vier Schlägen je Takt halten; dieses wird die Melodie freier machen und ihr sozusagen Flügel verleihen. Die Triolen im 3., 5., 7., 13. und 15. Takt sollten 'gemessen' sein; dieses sind mögliche

Lösungen: (Takt 3, 7, und 15) und

(Takt 5 und 13). Der Mittelteil muß mühelos

klingen (auch, wenn er es nicht ist!). Man sollte versuchen, die Triolenpassage *leggiero* zu spielen. Das Geheimnis besteht darin, die Zunge dahingehend zu üben, den Ton mit den kleinsten Bewegungen zu aktivieren; auf diese Weise können schnelle Wiederholungen die Lippenstellung nicht beeinträchtigen. Der Mundstückdruck sollte so leicht wie möglich sein; jede Reaktionsverminderung aufgrund taub gewordener Lippen hat einen negativen Einfluß auf den Klang.

15. Eine Zungenprüfung! Exakter Ton und präzise Artikulation sind wichtiger als äußerste Schnelligkeit im Spiel. Zungenstöße gegen die Zähne sind dabei behilflich. Versuch beides, den schnellen, einfachen und den langsamen, doppelten Zungenstoß; es ist wichtig, die Zungenstoßgeschwindigkeit ineinander übergehen zu lassen, so daß es nie zu einer halbschnellen Passage in der 'Lücke' zwischen den beiden Artikulationsarten kommt. Vorsicht bei den Passagen in tieferer Tonlage, damit die Zunge die Lippenöffnung nicht zu groß werden läßt; dies würde die Tonart verändern. (Das Zwerchfell durch die Bauchmuskeln zu stärken ist ebenfalls hilfreich.)

16. Obwohl Skryabins Präludium, op. 67, Nr. 1 durchweg ruhig und verhalten ist, benutzt es die gleiche harmonische Sprache und lebt in der gleichen mystischen, ekstatischen Welt wie das wohlbekannte *Poem of Ecstasy* (Gedicht der Ekstase) des Komponisten, einer der großen Marksteine auf dem Gebiet der Orchestertrompete. Technisch gesehen ist dieses Präludium eine *Legatoübung*, eine Übung in Atemkontrolle und des Spiels von äußerstem *pianissimo* und *dolcissimo*. Ein weicher Dämpfer wird hier empfohlen.

17. Ein lustiges Stück, das von dem amerikanischen Trompetenkomponisten George Gershwin beeinflußt wurde. Bei Musik dieser Art kann der Ton ruhig durch ein kontrolliertes *vibrato* "erwämt" werden. Der erste Teil ist lyrisch, und die Melodie sollte sich ungebrochen entfalten. Aber dennoch sollten die Achtelnoten peinlich genau gezählt werden, so daß eine exakte Übereinstimmung mit dem Klavierteil erfolgt. Im zweiten Teil (ab Takt 15) soll das Tempo gesteigert und zu einem ausdrucksvollen *rubato* gebracht werden.

18. Elgars Melodien eignen sich besonders gut für das Kornett, deshalb sollte ein süßer, kornettähnlicher Ton angestrebt werden. Man halte sich vor Augen, daß *nobilmente* eine von Elgars liebsten Anmerkungen für Blechpassagen war, aber auch, daß seine melodischen Kompositionen subtile Ausdrucksnuancen verlangen. Betonungszeichen können zu verschiedenen Perioden verschiedenes bedeuten; *sforzando* in Takt 34 verlangt eher scharfen Nachdruck als plötzlichen, starken Akzent.